This
Bible Verse Mapping
Book Belongs to:
_____

May the Lord bless your
Bible Verse Mapping Study time.

Bible Verse Mapping Instructions

There are many ways to do Bible Verse Mapping. These are simply guidelines to help you get started.

Step 1: Select a verse to map. Write it out in the "Verse" section of your page.

Step 2: Circle the keywords and any other words that you wish to define further. Look up the words in a Bible Dictionary (these are available online if you don't have one) and write the definitions in the "define" section of your page. Looking up the Greek or Hebrew meaning is a worthwhile addition to your study.

Step 3: Write the answers to any who, what, why and where questions you may have on the "explore" section.

Step 4: If you wish to research further, look up the verse in a few different translations and add any additional thoughts to your page.

Step 5: Write down any ways that the verse could be applied to your life today in the "application" section.

Step 6: Pray the verse. You can write the verse as a prayer in your own words in the "prayer" section or pray about the application you identified from the verse and how the Lord could use this in your life.

Bible Verse Mapping
Bonus Pages

There are 30 bonus pages in this Bible Verse Mapping and Study Book.

You may simply use them for an additional 30 days of Bible Verse Mapping or you may wish to use them for the days when all of the goodness of your study won't fit onto one page.

Bible Verse Mapping

Define

Verse

Explore

Application

Prayer

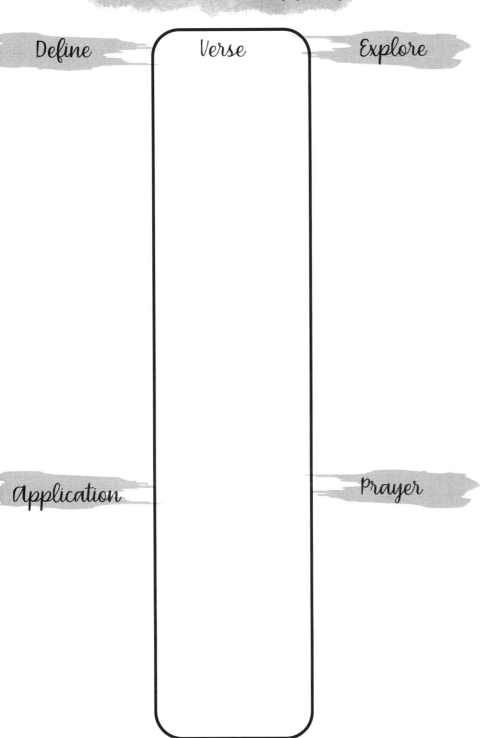

Bible Verse Mapping

Define

Verse

Explore

Application

Prayer

Bible Verse Mapping

Define

Verse

Explore

Application

Prayer

Bible Verse Mapping

Define

Verse

Explore

Application

Prayer

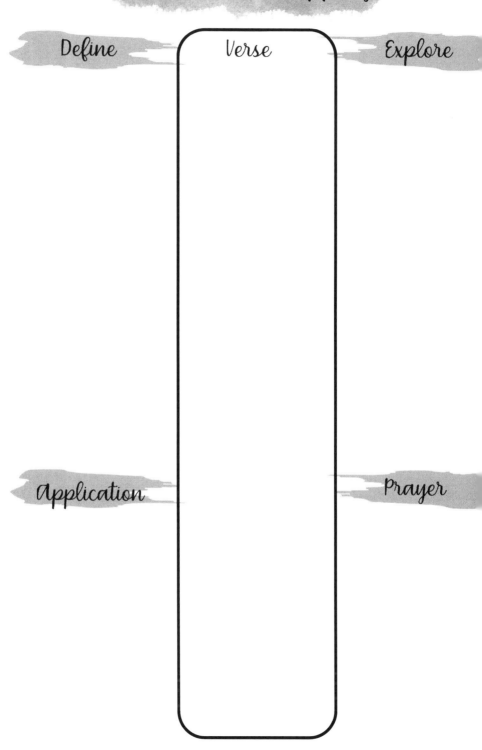

Bible Verse Mapping

Define

Verse

Explore

Application

Prayer

Bible Verse Mapping

Define

Verse

Explore

Application

Prayer

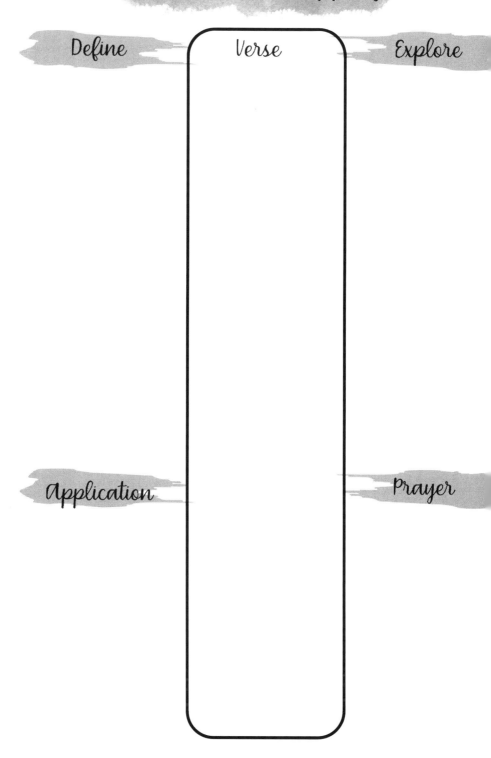

Bible Verse Mapping

Define

Verse

Explore

Application

Prayer

Bible Verse Mapping

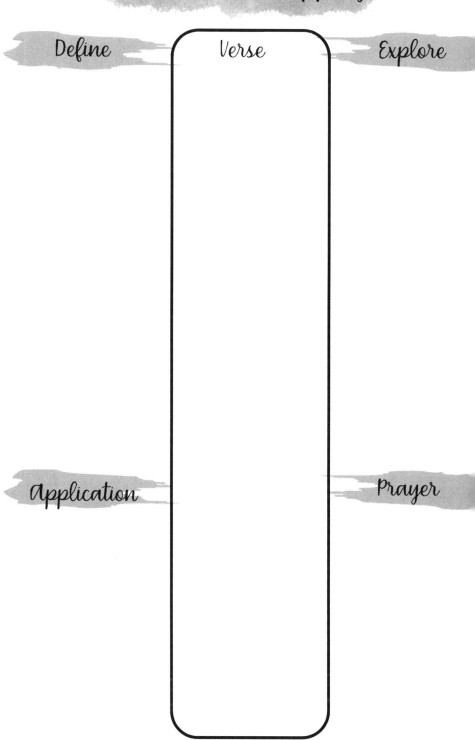

Define

Verse

Explore

Application

Prayer

Bible Verse Mapping

Define

Verse

Explore

Application

Prayer

Bible Verse Mapping

Define

Verse

Explore

Application

Prayer

Bible Verse Mapping

Define

Verse

Explore

Application

Prayer

Bible Verse Mapping

Define

Verse

Explore

Application

Prayer

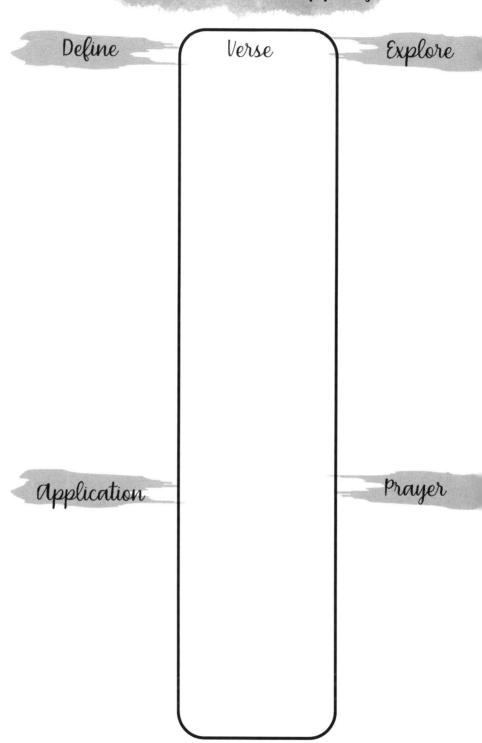

Bible Verse Mapping

Define

Verse

Explore

Application

Prayer

Bible Verse Mapping

Define

Verse

Explore

Application

Prayer

Bible Verse Mapping

Define

Verse

Explore

Application

Prayer

Bible Verse Mapping

Define

Verse

Explore

Application

Prayer

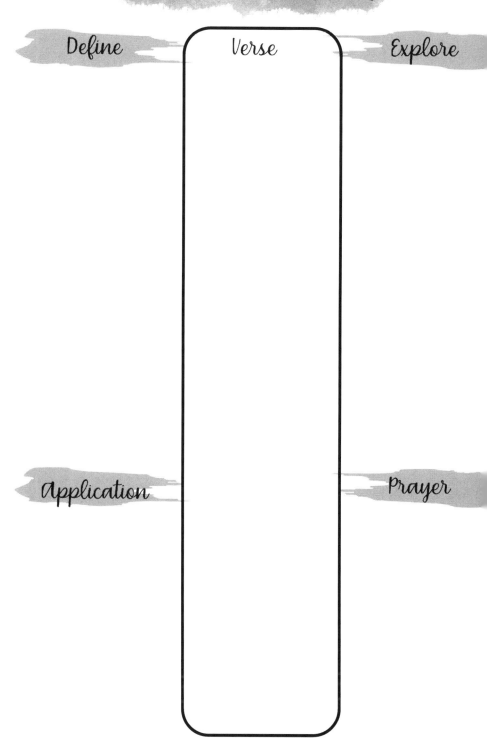

Bible Verse Mapping

Define

Verse

Explore

Application

Prayer

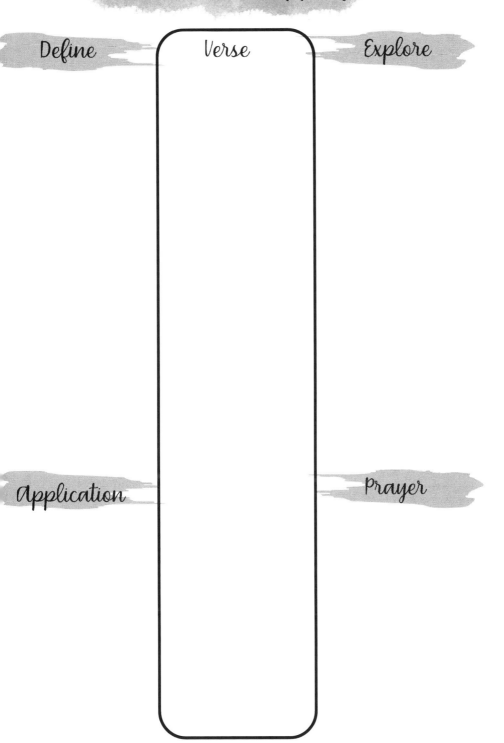

Bible Verse Mapping

Define

Verse

Explore

Application

Prayer

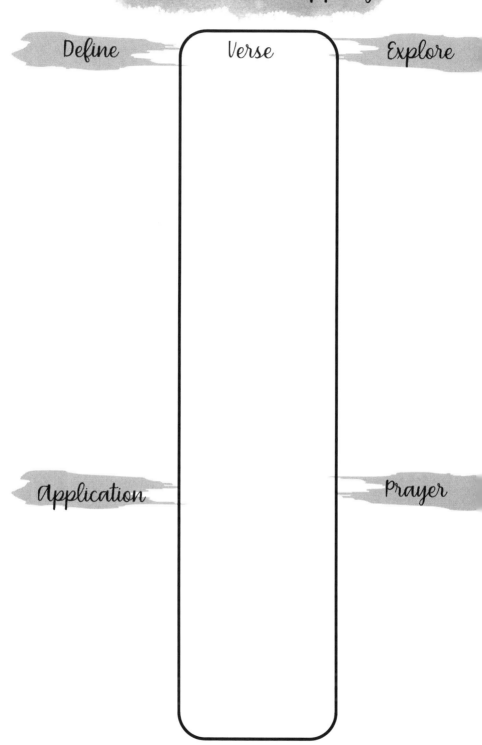

Bible Verse Mapping

Define

Verse

Explore

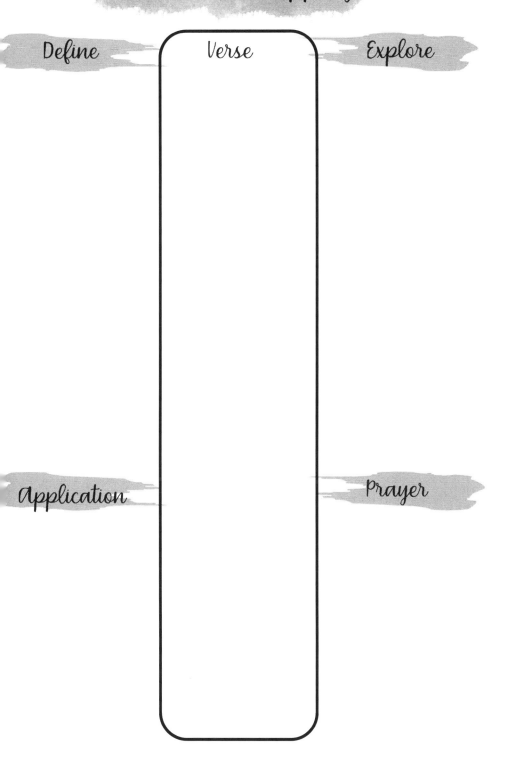

Application

Prayer

Bible Verse Mapping

Define

Verse

Explore

Application

Prayer

Bible Verse Mapping

Define

Verse

Explore

Application

Prayer

Bible Verse Mapping

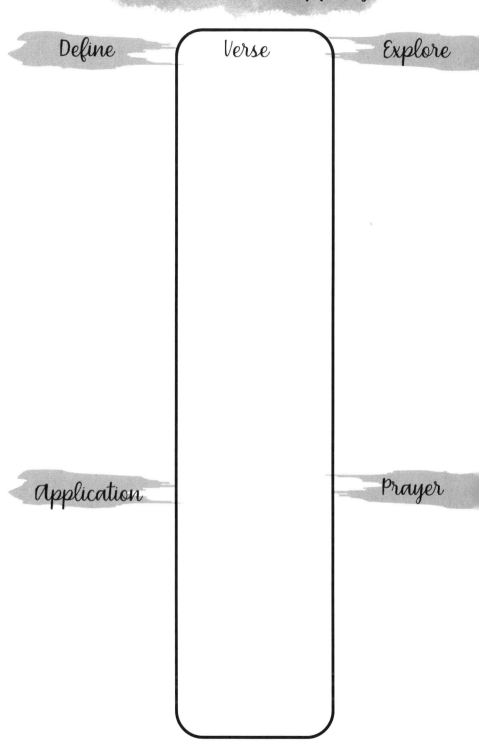

Define

Verse

Explore

Application

Prayer

Bible Verse Mapping

Define

Verse

Explore

Application

Prayer

Bible Verse Mapping

Define

Verse

Explore

Application

Prayer

Bible Verse Mapping

Define

Verse

Explore

Application

Prayer

Bible Verse Mapping

Define

Verse

Explore

Application

Prayer

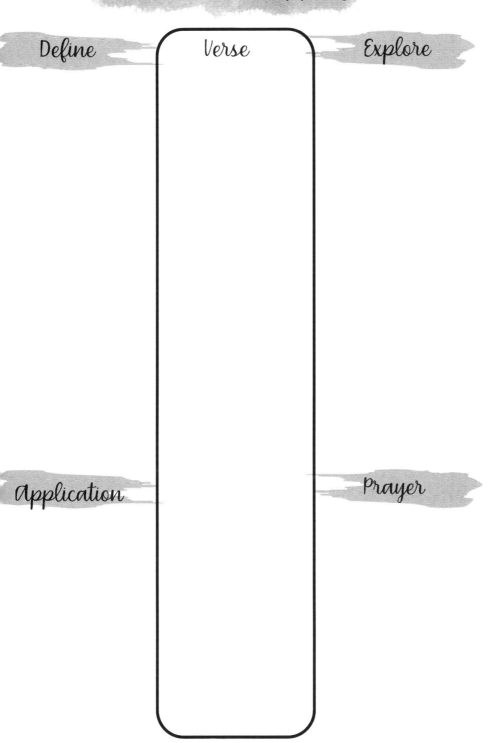

Bible Verse Mapping

Define

Verse

Explore

Application

Prayer

Bible Verse Mapping

Define

Verse

Explore

Application

Prayer

Bible Verse Mapping

Define

Verse

Explore

Application

Prayer

Bible Verse Mapping

Define

Verse

Explore

Application

Prayer

Bible Verse Mapping

Verse   Define

Explore

Application

Prayer

Bible Verse Mapping

Verse

Define

Explore

Application

Prayer

Bible Verse Mapping

Verse

Define

Explore

Application

Prayer

Bible Verse Mapping

Verse

Define

Explore

Application

Prayer

Bible Verse Mapping

Verse

Define

Explore

Application

Prayer

Bible Verse Mapping

Verse

Define

Explore

Application

Prayer

Bible Verse Mapping

Verse

Define

Explore

Application

Prayer

Bible Verse Mapping

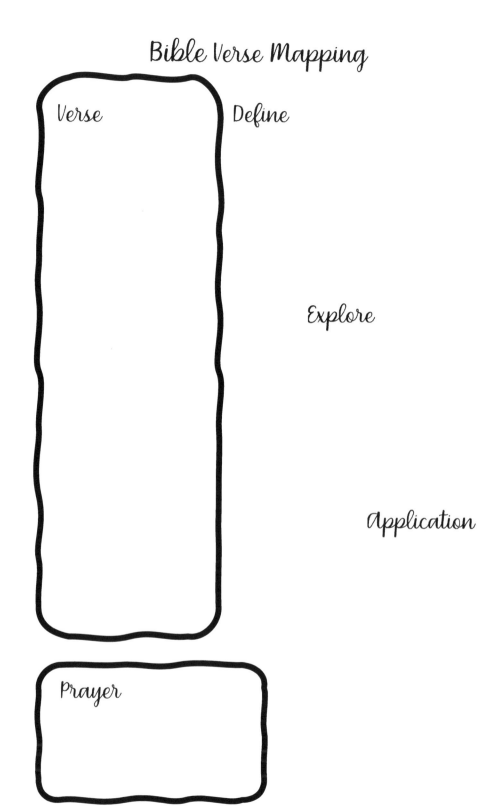

Verse

Define

Explore

Application

Prayer

Bible Verse Mapping

Verse

Define

Explore

Application

Prayer

Bible Verse Mapping

Verse

Define

Explore

Application

Prayer

Bible Verse Mapping

Verse

Define

Explore

Application

Prayer

Bible Verse Mapping

Verse

Define

Explore

Application

Prayer

Bible Verse Mapping

Verse

Define

Explore

Application

Prayer

Bible Verse Mapping

Verse

Define

Explore

Application

Prayer

Bible Verse Mapping

Verse

Define

Explore

Application

Prayer

Bible Verse Mapping

Verse

Define

Explore

Application

Prayer

Bible Verse Mapping

Verse

Define

Explore

Application

Prayer

Bible Verse Mapping

Verse

Define

Explore

Application

Prayer

Bible Verse Mapping

Verse

Define

Explore

Application

Prayer

Bible Verse Mapping

Verse

Define

Explore

Application

Prayer

Bible Verse Mapping

Verse

Define

Explore

Application

Prayer

Bible Verse Mapping

Verse

Define

Explore

Application

Prayer

Bible Verse Mapping

Verse

Define

Explore

Application

Prayer

Bible Verse Mapping

Verse

Define

Explore

Application

Prayer

Bible Verse Mapping

Verse

Define

Explore

Application

Prayer

Bible Verse Mapping

Verse   Define

Explore

Application

Prayer

Bible Verse Mapping

Verse

Define

Explore

Application

Prayer

Bible Verse Mapping

Verse

Define

Explore

Application

Prayer

Bible Verse Mapping

Verse

Define

Explore

Application

Prayer

Bible Verse Mapping

Verse

Define

Explore

Application

Prayer

Bible Verse Mapping

Define

Verse

Explore

Application

Prayer

Bible Verse Mapping

Define

Verse

Explore

Application

Prayer

Bible Verse Mapping

Define	Verse	Explore

Application

Prayer

Bible Verse Mapping

Define

Verse

Explore

Application

Prayer

Bible Verse Mapping

Define

Verse

Explore

Application

Prayer

Bible Verse Mapping

Define

Verse

Explore

Application

Prayer

Bible Verse Mapping

Define

Verse

Explore

Application

Prayer

Bible Verse Mapping

Define

Verse

Explore

Application

Prayer

Bible Verse Mapping

Define	Verse	Explore

Application

Prayer

Bible Verse Mapping

Define

Verse

Explore

Application

Prayer

Bible Verse Mapping

Define

Verse

Explore

Application

Prayer

Bible Verse Mapping

Define

Verse

Explore

Application

Prayer

Bible Verse Mapping

Define

Verse

Explore

Application

Prayer

Bible Verse Mapping

Define

Verse

Explore

Application

Prayer

Bible Verse Mapping

Define

Verse

Explore

Application

Prayer

Bible Verse Mapping

Define	Verse	Explore

Application

Prayer

Bible Verse Mapping

Define

Verse

Explore

Application

Prayer

Bible Verse Mapping

Define

Verse

Explore

Application

Prayer

Bible Verse Mapping

Define

Verse

Explore

Application

Prayer

Bible Verse Mapping

Define

Verse

Explore

Application

Prayer

Bible Verse Mapping

Define	Verse	Explore

Application

Prayer

Bible Verse Mapping

Define

Verse

Explore

Application

Prayer

Bible Verse Mapping

Define

Verse

Explore

Application

Prayer

Bible Verse Mapping

Define

Verse

Explore

Application

Prayer

Bible Verse Mapping

Define

Verse

Explore

Application

Prayer

Bible Verse Mapping

Define

Verse

Explore

Application

Prayer

Bible Verse Mapping

Define

Verse

Explore

Application

Prayer

Bible Verse Mapping

Define

Verse

Explore

Application

Prayer

Bible Verse Mapping

Define

Verse

Explore

Application

Prayer

Bible Verse Mapping

Define

Verse

Explore

Application

Prayer

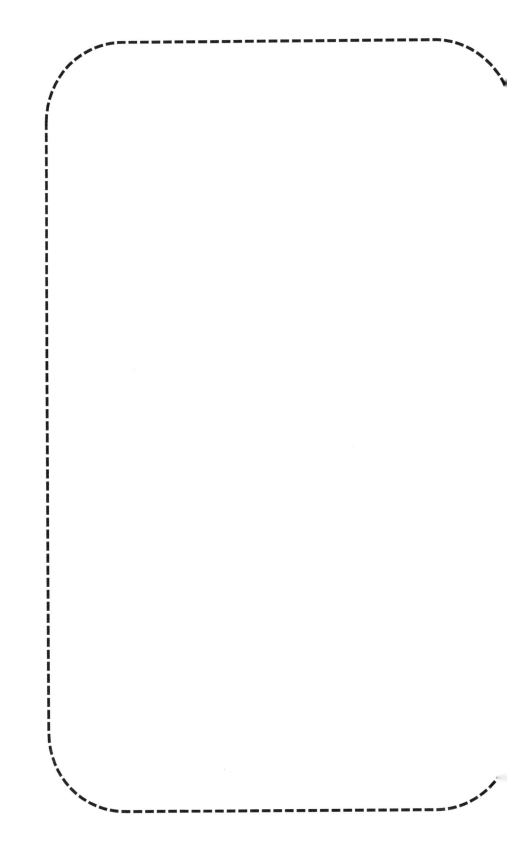

We hope you've enjoyed this
Bible Verse Mapping Book.

Be sure to check Amazon for
more faith-based books,
notebooks and workbooks
from our
Faith Anne Collection.

Printed in Great Britain
by Amazon

58801950R00072